CHINESE PHRASEBOOK

LEARN CHINESE QUICK AND EASY WITH CHINESE PHRASES

Zhang Jing

Table of Contents

GREETINGS – 问候

Hi

嗨

(hāi)

Goodbye

再见

(zàijiàn)

Long time no see!

好久不见！

(*hǎojiǔbujiàn*)

How is everything?

你好吗？

(nǐhǎo ma)

Good morning

早安

(zǎo'ān)

Good afternoon

午安

(wǔ'ān)

Good evening, good night

傍晚好，晚安

(bàngwǎn hǎo， wǎn'ān)

See you later

待会见

(dài huìjiàn)

Nice to meet you

很高兴认识你

(hěn gāoxìng rènshi nǐ)

Sorry

对不起

(duìbuqǐ)

Excuse me

不好意思

(bùhǎoyìsi)

Excitement & Emotions –情绪

It moved me

它打动了我

(tā dǎdòng le wǒ)

I'm very excited

我很兴奋

(wǒ hěn xīngfèn)

To be eager

迫不及待

(pòbùjídài)

To want

想要

(xiǎngyào)

Awesome!

太棒了!

(tài bàng le)

Cool!

酷!

(kù)

I choose this one

我选择这个

(wǒ xuǎnzé zhège)

That would be perfect!

这太好了！

(zhè tàihǎole)

Phenomenal!

惊人！

(jīngrén)

I'm going to cry

我快哭了

(wǒ kuài kū le)

How terrible

太糟了

(tài zāole)

What a shame

真丢脸

(zhēn diūliǎn)

Incredible!

不可思议！

(bùkěsīyì)

To look forward to something

很期待

(hěn qīdài)

I'm really looking forward to seeing it

我真的很期待看到它

(wǒ zhēn de hěn qīdài kàn dào tā)

To be in love

在爱里

(zài ài lǐ)

Mad

疯

(fēng)

Satisfied

满意

(mǎnyì)

Cheers!

干杯！

(gānbēi)

GETTING AROUND – 方向

High speed train

高速列车

(gāosù lièchē)

Travel

旅游

(lǚyóu)

Travel by...

用...旅游...

(yòng... lǚyóu...)

Subway

地铁

(dìtiě)

Intercity bus

城市间的巴士

(chéngshì jiān de bāshì)

Bus

巴士

(bāshì)

Transfer (bus, train, or subway)

转移（公共汽车，火车，或地铁）

(zhuǎnyí（gōnggòngqìchē, huǒchē, huò dìtiě）)

Transfer/connection/layover (plane)

转移/联系/短暂停留平面...

(zhuǎnyí/ liánxì/ duǎnzàn tíngliú píngmiàn...)

Fare

票价

(piàojià)

Walk around the neighborhood

散步在住宅区

(sànbù zài zhùzháiqū)

How do I get to...?

我如何去。。。?

(wǒ rúhé qù)

How long does it take to get there?

多久到达那儿？

(duōjiǔ dàodá nàr)

Over there

在那儿

(zàinar)

Can I walk there?

步行能到吗？

(bùxíng néng dào ma)

Let's get a taxi

让我们乘坐出租车

(ràng wǒmen chéngzuò chūzūchē)

Station

车站

(chēzhàn)

Stop (bus or subway)

车站(巴士或地铁）

(chēzhàn(bāshì huò dìtiě))

How many stops is it?

多少站？

(duōshao zhàn)

It's three stops away

三站的距离

(sān zhàn de jùlí)

Let's go on foot

让我们走路去吧

(ràng wǒmen zǒulù qù ba)

We'll take the subway

我们搭地铁

(wǒmen dā dìtiě)

COMMON VERBS –常用动词

To be able to

能够

(nénggòu)

I can

我可以

(wǒ kěyǐ)

To want

要

(yào)

I want

我要

(wǒ yào)

To need

需要

(xūyào)

I need

我需要

(wǒ xūyào)

To look for

寻找

(xúnzhǎo)

I look for

我寻找

(wǒ xúnzhǎo)

I'm looking for a place…

我在寻找一个地方

(wǒ zài xúnzhǎo yī gè dìfang)

To go

去

(qù)

I go

我去

(wǒ qù)

To have

有

(yǒu)

I have

我有

(wǒ yǒu)

I have to...

我需要

(wǒ xūyào)

To buy

买

(mǎi)

I buy

我买

(wǒ mǎi)

To dance

跳舞

(tiàowǔ)

I dance

我跳舞

(wǒ tiàowǔ)

To see

看

(kàn)

I see

我看

(wǒ kàn)

To help

帮

(bāng)

Help me, please

请帮我

(qǐng bāng wǒ)

To drive

驾驶

(jiàshǐ)

I drive

*我*驾驶

(wǒ jiàshǐ)

To take

拿

(ná)

I take

我拿

(wǒ ná)

To bring

带

(dài)

To get

拿

(ná)

To eat

吃

(chī)

I'm eating

我在吃

(wǒ zài chī)

To drink

喝

(hē)

I'm drinking

我在喝

(wǒ zài hē)

To do/to make

做

(zuò)

I do/I make

我做

(wǒ zuò)

To know (for skills and information)

知道 （技术和资料）

(zhīdào （ jìshù hé zīliào）)

I know

我知道

(wǒ zhīdào)

To know (knowledge about something or someone)

知道 (某人或某事的知识)

(zhīdào (mǒurén huò mǒushì de zhīshi))

I know

我知道

(wǒ zhīdào)

To start

开始

(kāishǐ)

I start

我开始

(wǒ kāishǐ)

To study

学习

(xuéxí)

I study

我学习

 (wǒ xuéxí)

To work

工作

(gōngzuò)

I work

我工作

(wǒ gōngzuò)

COMMON ADJECTIVES －常见的形容词

Well

行

(xíng)

Good

好

(hǎo)

Bad

坏

(huài)

Good looking

好看

(hǎokàn)

Pretty

漂亮

(piàoliang)

Beautiful

美

(měi)

Ugly

丑

(chǒu)

Cool, neat

整齐

(zhěngqí)

Brilliant

聪明

(cōngming)

Bright

亮

(liàng)

Dark

暗

(àn)

Happy

开心

(kāixīn)

Sad

伤心

(shāngxīn)

Tall

高

(gāo)

Short

矮

(ǎi)

Cheap

便宜

(piányi)

Expensive

贵

(guì)

Interesting

有趣

(yǒuqù)

Boring

闷

(mèn)

I'm tall

我很高

(wǒ hěn gāo)

I'm short

我很矮

(wǒ hěn ǎi)

Fat

肥

(féi)

Skinny

瘦

(shòu)

Fast

快

(kuài)

Slow

慢

(màn)

FOOD & DRINK – 饮食 & 饮料

What would you like to eat?

你想吃什么？

(nǐ xiǎng chī shénme)

What would you like to drink?

你想喝什么？

(nǐ xiǎng hē shénme)

I have a craving for...

我想吃。。。

(wǒ xiǎng chī)

What do you feel like having?

你想要什么？

(nǐ xiǎngyào shénme)

Enjoy your meal!

请享用！

(qǐng xiǎngyòng)

I'm hungry

我饿了

(wǒ è le)

Let's get a drink

让我们喝一杯

(ràng wǒmen hē yī bēi)

Do you want a drink?

你要喝一杯吗？

(nǐ yào hē yī bēi ma)

Drink (alcoholic)

饮料 （酒）

(yǐnliào （jiǔ）)

Soft drink

汽水

(qìshuǐ)

Homemade food

自家食物

(zìjiā shíwù)

Let's get tapas

让*我们小吃*

(ràng wǒmen xiǎochī)

To have breakfast

吃早餐

(chī zǎocān)

To have lunch

吃午餐

(chī wǔcān)

To have dinner

吃晚餐

(chī wǎncān)

Where are we going to have dinner?

哪里吃**晚餐**？

(nǎlǐ chī wǎncān)

Did you have breakfast already?

吃**早餐**了吗？

(chī zǎocān le ma)

What did you have for lunch?

你午餐吃什么？

(nǐ wǔcān chī shénme)

What is today's special?

今天**特别**是什么？

(jīntiān tèbié shì shénme)

Where did you have dinner?

你在哪里吃了晚餐？

(nǐ zài nǎlǐ chī le wǎncān)

For here or to go?

这里吃或带走？

(zhèlǐ chī huò dàizǒu)

Take away

打包

(dǎbāo)

Meat

肉

(ròu)

Chicken

鸡

(jī)

Fish

鱼

(yú)

Fruit

水果

(shuǐguǒ)

Vegetables

蔬菜

(shūcài)

Salad

沙拉

(shālā)

Sandwich

三明治

(sānmíngzhì)

Coffee (with milk)

咖啡 （奶）

(kāfēi （nǎi）)

Tea (with milk)

茶 （奶）

(chá （nǎi）)

Afternoon snack

下午小吃

(xiàwǔ xiǎochī)

Do I need a reservation?

需要订座吗？

(xūyào dìng zuò ma)

Can I see the menu?

可以看菜单吗？

(kěyǐ kàn càidān ma)

What do you recommend?

你推荐哪儿？

(nǐ tuījiàn nǎr)

Where is a good restaurant?

哪里有好餐厅?

(nǎlǐ yǒu hǎo cāntīng)

Do you know a good place to eat?

你知道好吃的地方吗?

(nǐ zhīdào hǎochī de dìfang ma)

I'm a vegetarian

我是素食

(wǒ shì sùshí)

I'm a vegan

我是一个素食主义者

(wǒ shì yī gè sùshízhǔyì zhě)

I can't have…

我不能要。。。

(wǒ bùnéng yào)

I'm allergic to…

我对。。。过敏

(wǒ duì。。。 guòmǐn)

I'm allergic to nuts/ seafood
我对豆类/海鲜过敏

(wǒ duì dòulèi/ hǎixiān guòmǐn)

I'm lactose intolerant
我有乳糖不耐症

(wǒ yǒu rǔtángbùnàizhèng)

What are today's specials?

什么是今天的特色菜？

(shénme shì jīntiān de tèsè cài)

I'd like to try a regional dish

我想尝试当地的菜

(wǒ xiǎng chángshì dāngdì de cài)

TRAVELING – 旅游

To travel

旅游

(lǚyóu)

A trip

旅程

(lǚchéng)

Have a good trip!

玩的开心！

(wán de kāixīn)

How much is a taxi to the airport?

的士去机场多少钱？

(dīshì qù jīchǎng duōshao qián)

Airport

机场

(jīchǎng)

Airplane

飞机

(fēijī)

I'm traveling

我在旅游

(wǒ zài lǚyóu)

Flight

飞机程

(fēijī chéng)

What time is your flight?

你的飞机几点?

(nǐ de fēijī jǐdiǎn)

What time do you get in?

你几点进去?

(nǐ jǐdiǎn jìnqù)

I missed my flight

我错过飞机了

(wǒ cuòguò fēijī le)

Delay

延迟

(yánchí)

Check if your flight is delayed

检查你的飞机有延迟吗

(jiǎnchá nǐ de fēijī yǒu yánchí ma)

When do we land?

*几点**降临**？*

(jǐdiǎn jiànglín)

I've lost my passport

我不见护照

(wǒ bùjiàn hùzhào)

Here is my passport

这是我的护照

(zhè shì wǒ de hùzhào)

How are you getting to Barcelona?

如何去巴塞罗那？

(rúhé qù Bāsàiluónà)

We're going by train

我们搭火车去

(wǒmen dā huǒchē qù)

I'm here on business

我是为生意而来

(wǒ shì wéi shēngyì ér lái)

I'm here on vacation

我来*旅行*

(wǒ lái lǚxíng)

I'm going on vacation

我去*旅行*

(wǒ qù lǚxíng)

I'm here for the weekend

我来*度过周末*

(wǒ lái dùguò zhōumò)

I'll be here two weeks

我来*两个星期*

(wǒ lái liǎng gè xīngqī)

Tickets

票

(piào)

Boarding pass

登机卡

(dēngjī kǎ)

When do you leave?

你几时离开？

(nǐ jǐshí líkāi)

HOTEL – 酒店

I have a reservation

我有预约

(wǒ yǒu yùyuē)

I don't have a reservation

我没有预约

(wǒ méiyǒu yùyuē)

I will be staying one week

我在这一个星期

(wǒ zài zhè yī gè xīngqī)

I'd like a single room

我要单人房

(wǒ yào dānrén fáng)

We'd like a room with a double bed

我要单房，双人床

(wǒ yào dān fáng,　shuāngrénchuáng)

Please give me a wake up call tomorrow at 8 a.m.

明天早上8点叫醒我

(míngtiān zǎoshang8 diǎn jiàoxǐng wǒ)

Our room hasn't been cleaned

我们的房间没有被清理

(wǒmen de fángjiān méiyǒu bèi qīnglǐ)

The air conditioning isn't working

冷气机坏了

(lěngqìjī huàile)

I'm ready to check-out

我已经准备好退房

(wǒ yǐjīng zhǔnbèi hǎo tuìfáng)

Can I check the bill, please?

可以检查账单吗？

(kěyǐ jiǎnchá zhàngdān ma)

I'm looking for a guest staying here

我在需找一个客人

(wǒ zài xū zhǎo yī gè kèrén)

I'm going to stay at the Hilton

我会留在希尔顿

(wǒ huì liú zài Xī'ěrdùn)

Is there still room service?

是否还有客房服务

(shìfǒu háiyǒu kèfáng fúwù)

We're looking for a cheap room

我们在找便宜的房间

(wǒmen zài zhǎo piányi de fángjiān)

Are there any vacant rooms?

有没有空置房

(yǒu méiyǒu kōngzhì fáng)

Is breakfast included?

有包括早餐吗？

(yǒu bāokuò zǎocān ma)

Can I have the bill please?

我要账单

(wǒ yào zhàngdān)

I'm ready to check out

我准备退房

(wǒ zhǔnbèi tuìfáng)

I'll pay with card

我用卡付账

(wǒ yòng kǎ fùzhàng)

I need my room cleaned

我要我的房被清理

(wǒ yào wǒ de fáng bèi qīnglǐ)

Sorry, we're full

对不起，满了

(duìbuqǐ,   mǎn le)

HELP – 救

Can you help me please?

你可以**帮我**吗？

(nǐ kěyǐ bāng wǒ ma)

Can you lend me a hand?

可以**帮我一下**吗？

(kěyǐ bāng wǒ yīxià ma)

Have you been helped?

你得到**帮助了吗**？

(nǐ dédào bāngzhù le ma)

To assist

协助

(xiézhù)

Can I help you?

*如何**帮到你**?*

(rúhé bāng dào nǐ)

How can I help you?

*我如何**帮到你**?*

(wǒ rúhé bāng dào nǐ)

To lend/loan

借

(jiè)

Can you lend me some money?

你可以**借我一点**钱吗？

(nǐ kěyǐ jiè wǒ yīdiǎn qián ma)

Can I borrow your car?

可以**借我你的**车吗？

(kěyǐ jiè wǒ nǐ de chē ma)

Can I get you anything?

我可以给你什么吗？

(wǒ kěyǐ gěi nǐ shénme ma)

Do you need any help?

你需要**帮忙**吗？

(nǐ xūyào bāngmáng ma)

NIGHTLIFE – 夜生活

To go out

出去

(chūqù)

Are you going out tonight?

*你今晚出去*吗？

(nǐ jīnwǎn chūqù ma)

We're going to have some drinks

我们将喝一些

(wǒmen jiāng hē yīxiē)

To go out all night/go out hard

出门一整夜

(chūmén yī zhěngyè)

Bar hop

酒吧跃

(jiǔbā yuè)

What do you want to drink?

你要喝什么？

(nǐ yào hē shénme)

Nightclub

夜店

(yèdiàn)

Party

派对

(pàiduì)

Huge party

大型派对

(dàxíng pàiduì)

Beer please

请给我啤酒

(qǐng gěi wǒ píjiǔ)

We're going out tonight

我们今晚出去

(wǒmen jīnwǎn chūqù)

Let's go somewhere else

*我们**去**别的地方*

(wǒmen qù biéde dìfang)

Do you like to dance?

*你要**跳舞**吗？*

(nǐ yào tiàowǔ ma)

We're going out hard

*我们**玩**疯*

(wǒmen wán fēng)

Tipsy

喝醉

(hēzuì)

Drunk

醉

(zuì)

RUNNING ERRANDS —外出办事

What time do you open?

你几点开门?

(nǐ jǐdiǎn kāimén)

What time do you close?

你几点关门?

(nǐ jǐdiǎn guānmén)

Are you open Sundays?

星期日有开吗?

(Xīngqīrì yǒu kāi ma)

How much do I owe you?

我欠你多少?

(wǒ qiàn nǐ duōshao)

Can I pay with card?

我可以用卡付费吗?

(wǒ kěyǐ yòng kǎ fùfèi ma)

Can I have a receipt?

我可以拿收据吗?

(wǒ kěyǐ ná shōujù ma)

Could you give me...?

你可以可我。。。吗?

(nǐ kěyǐ kě wǒ。。。 ma)

Can you deliver it to my hotel?

*你可以**送去酒店**吗？*

(nǐ kěyǐ sòngqù jiǔdiàn ma)

Thank you

谢谢

(xiè xie)

TIME – 时间

It's one o'clock

现在是一点钟

(xiànzài shì yīdiǎn zhōng)

It's two o'clock

现在是两点钟

 (xiànzài shì liǎng diǎnzhōng)

It's noon

现在是中午

(xiànzài shì zhōngwǔ)

It's midnight

现在是半夜

(xiànzài shì bànyè)

It's 3:05

现在是三点零五分

(xiànzài shì sān diǎn líng wǔ fēn)

It's 2:30

现在是两点半

(xiànzài shì liǎng diǎn bàn)

It's 4:45

现在是四点四十五分

(xiànzài shì sì diǎn sì shíwǔ fēn)

It's 8:15

现在是八点十五分

(xiànzài shì bā diǎn shíwǔ fēn)

It's 10:50

现在是十点五十分

(xiànzài shì shí diǎn wǔshí fēn)

It's late

迟了

(chíle)

It's still early

现在还早

(xiànzài hái zǎo)

Soon

快了

(kuài le)

Early

早了

(zǎo le)

Late

迟

*(*chí*)*

In the morning

早上

(zǎoshang)

In the afternoon

下午

(xiàwǔ)

In the evening

傍晚

(bàngwǎn)

At night

晚上

(wǎnshang)

Yesterday

昨天

(zuótiān)

Tomorrow

明天

(míngtiān)

I'll see you tomorrow morning

明早见

(míngzǎo jiàn)

Tomorrow afternoon

明天**下午**

(míngtiān xiàwǔ)

Tomorrow evening

明天傍晚

(míngtiān bàngwǎn)

Tomorrow night

明天晚上

(míngtiān wǎnshang)

At what time?

几点？

(jǐdiǎn)

Since what time?

从几时?

(cóng jǐshí)

An hour ago

一小时前

(yī xiǎoshí qián)

What time does it start?

*几时**开始**？*

(jǐshí kāishǐ)

DATING & FLIRTING – 约会

Go out with someone

和人出去

(hé rén chūqù)

To cheat

骗

(piàn)

Third Wheel

第三者

(dìsānzhě)

To make out

亲热

(qīnrè)

One-night stand

一夜情

(yīyèqíng)

To have a one-night stand

一夜情

(yīyèqíng)

To be in a relationship with someone

和人有关系

(hé rén yǒuguān xì)

My treat!

我请你

(wǒ qǐng nǐ)

To be engaged

订婚

(dìnghūn)

Are you married?

你结婚了吗？

(nǐ jiéhūn le ma)

Do you have a boyfriend?

你有**男友**吗？

(nǐ yǒu nányǒu ma)

Do you have a girlfriend?

你有**女友**吗？

(nǐ yǒu nǚyǒu ma)

What do you do?

你干什么？

(nǐ gànshénme)

COMMON QUESTIONS – 常见问题

What's your name?

你叫**什么名**?

(nǐ jiào shénme míng)

Where are you from?

你**哪里来**?

(nǐ nǎlǐ lái)

How long have you been here?

你在**那多久了**?

(nǐ zài nà duōjiǔ le)

Do you speak Spanish?

你会说西班牙语吗？

(nǐ huì shuō Xībānyáyǔ ma)

Do you speak English?

你说英文吗？

 (nǐ shuō Yīngwén ma)

Where do you work?

你在哪里工作？

(nǐ zài nǎlǐ gōngzuò)

Are you studying?

你还在读书吗？

(nǐ hái zài dúshū ma)

Where do you live?

你住哪儿？

(nǐ zhù nǎr)

What are your hobbies?

你的爱好是什么？

(nǐ de àihào shì shénme)

Do you like soccer?

你喜欢足球吗？

(nǐ xǐhuan zúqiú ma)

How's your family?

你的家人如何？

(nǐ de jiārén rúhé)

Do you have any siblings?

你有*兄弟姐妹*吗？

(nǐ yǒu xiōngdì jiěmèi ma)

Where are you going?

你去*哪儿*？

(nǐ qù nǎr)

What are you doing?

你在*做什么*？

(nǐ zài zuò shénme)

What music do you like?

你喜欢*什么 音乐*？

(nǐ xǐhuan shénme yīnyuè)

Does it scare you?

吓到你了吗？

(xià dào nǐ le ma)

Are you in a hurry?

你赶时间吗？

(nǐ gǎn shíjiān ma)

Do you like it?

你喜欢吗？

(nǐ xǐhuan ma)

How do you say... in Spanish?

...在西班牙怎么 说?

(... zài Xībānyá zěnme shuō)

SLANG – 腔调

Amazing (vulgar)

好

(hǎo)

Drunk

醉

(zuì)

A great deal

好生意

(hǎo shēngyì)

Guy

男的

(nánde)

Friend/Dude

朋友

(péngyou)

Great time

好时间

(hǎo shíjiān)

Messed up

搞砸了

(gǎozá le)

A mess

状况

(zhuàngkuàng)

Strong/buff

强壮

(qiángzhuàng)

To speak in simple terms

简单来说

(jiǎndān láishuō)

To pull someone's leg

开玩笑

(kāiwánxiào)

Goofy

傻傻的

(shǎ shǎ de)

Very stupid

笨死了

(bèn sǐ le)

Soulmate

天生一对

(tiānshēng yīduì)

Good for nothing

没用

(méiyòng)

Piece of cake

简单

(jiǎndān)

All talk

说罢了

(shuō bàle)

Small world

小世界

(xiǎo shìjiè)

Beggars can't be choosers

求人不能选择

(qiúrén bùnéng xuǎnzé)

I'm in a rush

我赶时间

(wǒ gǎn shíjiān)

To work

工作

(gōngzuò)

I work, a job

我有工作

(wǒ yǒu gōngzuò)

WEATHER – 天气

How's the weather?

天气如何？

(tiānqì rúhé)

It's cold

冷

(lěng)

It's cool

酷

(kù)

It's hot

热

(rè)

It's so hot!

好热

(hǎo rè)

It's so cold!

好冷

(hǎo lěng)

It's windy

多风

(duō fēng)

The weather's bad

天气糟糕

(tiānqì zāogāo)

It's humid

潮湿

(cháoshī)

It's sunny

有阳光

(yǒu yángguāng)

It's nice out

户外好

(hùwài hǎo)